34 Stories
That Explain Personal Finance

FOLLOWING SALLY'S
PERSONAL FINANCE JOURNEY

34 Stories That Explain Personal Finance

KEN BOYD
author of *The CPA Exam for Dummies*

Copyright © 2024 by Ken Boyd

All rights reserved.

No portion of this book may be reproduced in any form without written permission from the publisher or author, except as permitted by U.S. copyright law.

This publication is designed to provide accurate and authoritative information in regard to the subject matter covered. It is sold with the understanding that neither the author nor the publisher is engaged in rendering legal, investment, accounting or other professional services. While the publisher and author have used their best efforts in preparing this book, they make no representations or warranties with respect to the accuracy or completeness of the contents of this book and specifically disclaim any implied warranties of merchantability or fitness for a particular purpose. No warranty may be created or extended by sales representatives or written sales materials. The advice and strategies contained herein may not be suitable for your situation. You should consult with a professional when appropriate. Neither the publisher nor the author shall be liable for any loss of profit or any other commercial damages, including but not limited to special, incidental, consequential, personal, or other damages.

Paperback ISBN: 979-8-218-54604-5
eBook ISBN: 979-8-218-54605-2

Book Design by *the*BookDesigners
Cover images © Shutterstock

First edition 2024

I dedicate this book to my father, Bill Boyd, who was a hero to me. This book is also dedicated to my closest friend, my wife Patty, and our children. Finally, this book is dedicated to the faculty and staff of three St. Louis schools: Chaminade College Preparatory School, St. Peter Catholic School in Kirkwood, and Visitation Academy. Thank you for educating my children.

Table of Contents

1	CHAPTER 1	Why I wrote this book
5	CHAPTER 2	Obstacles to learning personal finance
9	CHAPTER 3	How complexity harms investors
15	CHAPTER 4	Delayed gratification and needs vs. wants
18	CHAPTER 5	Creating a monthly budget
22	CHAPTER 6	Compounding interest and the Rule of 72
27	CHAPTER 7	Reconciling your bank account
30	CHAPTER 8	Recovering from a financial setback
35	CHAPTER 9	Understanding common stocks
39	CHAPTER 10	How stocks are traded
43	CHAPTER 11	Common stock returns
47	CHAPTER 12	Understanding bond investing
51	CHAPTER 13	Mutual fund investing options
55	CHAPTER 14	Understanding retirement plans
58	CHAPTER 15	Selecting an investment advisor
63	CHAPTER 16	Reviewing common investing mistakes
68	CHAPTER 17	Asset allocation models
72	CHAPTER 18	Why earnings per share is important
76	CHAPTER 19	Stock dividends, and shareholder returns
79	CHAPTER 20	Preferred stock and convertible securities
81	CHAPTER 21	Realized gains and recognized gains

84	CHAPTER 22	Stock index gains and losses
88	CHAPTER 23	Investment objectives
91	CHAPTER 24	Mutual fund costs
94	CHAPTER 25	Mutual fund performance
97	CHAPTER 26	Exchange-traded funds
100	CHAPTER 27	Bond mutual funds
103	CHAPTER 28	Working with bond premiums and bond discounts
106	CHAPTER 29	The importance of credit scores
109	CHAPTER 30	Unexpected credit card fees
112	CHAPTER 31	Reviewing taxes on investments
117	CHAPTER 32	Tax deduction limitations
121	CHAPTER 33	The myth of cheap insurance
125	CHAPTER 34	Reviewing the personal finance journey

CHAPTER 1

Why I Wrote This Book

There are too many successful, intelligent people who don't have a playbook to learn personal finance.

That's why.

You may have an advanced degree and work as an expert in your field but never spend much time thinking about personal finances — until you're forced to. Here are some examples:

- A therapist who is managing her own practice. Holds a graduate degree and professional credentials. Frustrated with the process of filing her tax return.

- The Yale-educated doctor and researcher who is told by her realtor that "mortgage interest is 100% deductible on your tax return". Her CPA explains that isn't accurate. (In past years, the deduction was limited, based on total gross income).

- VP of marketing with a Harvard MBA who is presented three different proposals for life insurance and doesn't understand how they differ.

All people I know personally. Highly educated and successful people who could make better personal finance decisions if someone gave them a playbook.

I hope that this book meets that need.

FORMAT AND STYLE

I've made decisions about the book's format and style to (hopefully) keep your attention, and to make the book more digestible.

STORY-BASED EXAMPLES

My Accounting Accidentally Substack content introduces finance and accounting concepts with a story. Here's an example:

"Save 100% When You Don't Buy Anything: Opportunity Costs and Compounding Interest"

I saw a meme of a sign outside a store that said: "Save 100% When You Don't Buy Anything". I thought it was funny and a useful way to introduce opportunity costs and compounding interest (both topics are covered later).

Now, had I just launched into these finance topics without the story, you might not keep reading.

As often as possible, I start a new topic with a story that I hope will keep you engaged. After all, my goal is to motivate you to keep reading, so you can use what's in the book.

ONE EXAMPLE THROUGHOUT THE BOOK

This book will follow the personal finances of Sally and the decisions she makes along the way. You'll see her personal budget, the investment decisions she makes, and other information.

By using one example and building on it, you can visualize how the decisions fit together. For example:

- The monthly budget she creates early in the book impacts the amount she invests each month.

- The retirement plan she has through work impacts how she invests. She chooses stock and bond investments offered within the retirement plan.

You can always refer back to other sections of the book to refresh your memory about Sally's decisions.

INFORMATION IN SMALL AMOUNTS

As I introduce new concepts, the information will be in small amounts. For example, there are thousands of mutual funds to choose from.

I'm going to explain just a few.

Understanding mutual funds is challenging- I'll minimize the complexity by using a limited number of examples.

ACTION STEPS YOU CAN TAKE

I hope that you do something with the information in this book — that you'll take action.

You'll see many suggestions for what to do next: create a budget, reconcile your bank account monthly (many people don't), and talk to an investment advisor and/or a CPA.

Again, this is meant to be a playbook that motivates you to take some initial steps to improve your personal finances.

Ok, ready?

There are several obstacles to learning and understanding personal finance.

CHAPTER 2

Obstacles to Learning Personal Finance

Change — any change — is hard, and we all have too many choices.

CHANGE IS HARD

"To improve is to change; to be perfect is to change often"
—WINSTON CHURCHILL

In 2017, Trinidad and Tobago (a country of slightly less than 1.4 million people) beat the US Men's Soccer Team (325 million people) to eliminate the US from the World Cup soccer tournament. Back then, we Americans got excited about a new coach, new team members- and we didn't seem to make much progress in Men's soccer.

Serious change was needed- more than the status quo.

The US Women's Team, on the other hand, won the World Cup in 2015 and 2019- proof that the US *could* figure out international soccer.

The reason that people don't diet, don't exercise, and don't resolve bad personal relationships is that change is hard. As a result, we don't truly change and grow unless we're in real pain. When we're at that point, the pain of change is less severe than the pain of **not changing**.

But the fact remains — change is really hard.

TOO MANY CHOICES

All I needed was deodorant.

The exact type was Dove Men+Care Extra Fresh, gray packaging with a light green square on the label. I've used it for years.

When I got to Target, I was faced with a tsunami of choices. Dove alone had dozens of deodorant options, and the differences in packaging were only slight.

I had to lie down in the aisle, take a nap, and then make a choice.

OK, I'm lying about the nap, but I'm sure you've experienced the same thing. We have far too many choices with *everything*: food, clothing, entertainment, business products, and tools.

ISN'T IT ALL DOG FOOD?

According to The American Pet Product Association 2017-2018 Pet Ownership Survey "68% of US households own a pet and spend an average of $300 annually on pet food and treats. The US pet food market is expected to reach $30 billion in 2022."

That's a lot of Alpo. Believe it or not, the Tonight Show used to run live commercials for Alpo. They'd have a dog on set eating out of a bowl- you can find clips on YouTube.

Another quote from the same source: "Pet food and treat options available to US pet owners have exploded in recent years. GfK reports the number of brands has increased 71% since 2011 and now totals 630."

Really? 630 brands?

There's a term that describes this issue: the paradox of choice.

LOTS OF CHOICES ISN'T A GREAT THING

"The paradox of choice stipulates that while we might believe that being presented with multiple options actually makes it easier to choose one that we are happy with, and thus increases consumer satisfaction, having an abundance of options actually requires more effort to make a decision and can leave us feeling unsatisfied with our choice."

Deciding between multiple options requires more time and more distractions. The quote continues:

"When the number of choices increases, so does the difficulty of knowing what is best. Instead of increasing our freedom to have what we want, the paradox of choice suggests that having too many choices actually limits our freedom."

Many people believe that having dozens (or hundreds) of choices is a good thing. Turns out it may not be.

Not sure if you buy the argument? Think about investing.

CHAPTER 3

How Complexity Harms Investors

Complexity is harming investors.

This quote from a CNBC article from April of 2022 starts to explain why:

"As more cutting-edge investment products work their way into the marketplace, there's growing fear retail investors and even professional brokers are getting in over their heads."

Note the end of the sentence- it's important. Investing may now be too complex for *professional brokers*, those who manage investments for a living. Complex product offerings are part of the problem:

"The Financial Industry Regulatory Authority, or FINRA, considers leveraged and inverse ETFs, equity-indexed annuities and reverse convertibles as complex products."

I was in the investment business for years. I stay informed and I've never heard of an inverse EFT. I guess the joke is on me...

THOUSANDS OF CHOICES

Consider this: The more investment choices there are, the more your investment advisor must learn- and monitor- to stay informed. So how many investment choices are out there?

Mutual funds — they're straightforward, right?

Over the past 40 years, individual investors have used mutual funds with great success. However, Statista reported that there were 7,222 mutual funds as of 2023.

What about exchange-traded funds (ETFs)- another investment product used by individual investors? Statista reported 3,243 ETFs in the US in 2023.

Warren Buffet, possibly the world's most successful investor, says "Don't invest in businesses you don't understand." It's hard to make decisions and understand your investments with so many choices.

Is your insurance agent or CPA soliciting your investment business? You're not alone.

TOO MANY ADVISORS

In the late 90s and early 2000s, I trained over 1,000 people in a test prep course to become licensed as investment advisors through FINRA, the regulatory agency. I worked for a company that is now part of Kaplan, and I taught a 40-hour course once a month (one of the hardest things

I've ever done).

Many of the people in my classes were CPAs and insurance agents who were moving into the investment advisory field. This trend creates confusion for investors because professionals in other fields are now licensed as investment advisors.

Wait, I thought Bob was an insurance agent — why is he asking about my retirement plan?

Not making a decision *is a decision*. If we simply pass on making a decision, our problems can compound and get worse.

PROBLEMS COMPOUND: AN EXAMPLE

"He can't lick his butt — that's why he's got an infection and losing weight."

I hope she's talking about a dog, I thought.

As I walked by and heard more of the phone call, it turned out that the woman was a vet, and she was on the phone with a client.

Both humans and animals often have medical complications- one issue can snowball into multiple problems. For example, a patient has bad teeth and doesn't eat well. He loses weight and starts having problems related to poor nutrition.

Problems compound- and we all should avoid compounding problems when dealing with personal finances.

Let's move to a discussion of your personal finance goals.

WHAT ARE YOUR GOALS?

Here are some examples that may apply to you:

- I want to make smarter decisions about spending (not let money fall through my fingers).

- Covering unexpected expenses is frustrating. I need an emergency fund to pay for car repairs and other surprises.

- My goal is to buy a home or apartment in five years. I need to save and invest for a down payment.

- I'd like to retire in 20 years, and I need an investment fund to cover expenses in retirement.

Setting up an emergency fund may be a short-term goal while funding retirement is a long-term goal.

WHY GOALS MATTER

The reason why you're reading this book is to help you reach your goals. That's the payoff for putting in the time and effort to learn about personal finances.

So, when the process feels difficult, remember your goals.

Having goals also gives you direction, and that helps you stick to your goals.

Why am I not spending more on a vacation this year?

Oh, that's right: I committed to saving more money for a house down payment.

KEEP YOUR HEAD- EVEN WHEN EVERYONE AROUND YOU IS LOSING THEIRS

Markets are volatile, and goals help you remain consistent when markets are rapidly declining- or skyrocketing higher.

When markets are up, it may seem like everyone around you is getting rich- but that's normal. In every bull market (periods with higher stock prices) I've seen since the '87 market crash, most of us think everyone is making a pile of money.

No one wants to feel left out, right?

But there's a trade-off. As you'll learn later, the people who are killing it in the markets are probably taking more risk.

You need to keep your head and realize that your goals haven't changed.

34 STORIES THAT EXPLAIN PERSONAL FINANCE

Bull markets, historically, come to an end at some point. In other words, stock prices don't go up forever.

It's as Tom Petty sang: "The waiting is the hardest part."

Do you benefit from being patient? Read on...

CHAPTER 4

Delayed Gratification and Needs vs. Wants

With discipline and time, I think most people can accumulate far more wealth than they think is possible. But growing wealth requires change- which is precisely why most people don't make the effort. The changes I'm suggesting involve an old friend:

DELAYED GRATIFICATION

Some decisions are relatively small:

- Dropping a subscription music service and just listening to the free version (Pandora, for example).

- Making coffee at home two days a week and buying Starbucks less often.

- Buying more generic products when you go to the grocery store and Target. (I'm not going generic on salad dressing, however).

Since these are smaller decisions, the amount of gratification you're delaying is small. You don't mind listening to the commercials on Pandora (I certainly don't- I just turned down the sound), and the coffee at home isn't bad.

Other decisions are much bigger. Several years ago, StudySoup wrote a great article on the average amount of money a college student saves by having a roommate. The average savings over four years was over $15,000.

Now, having a roommate is a big sacrifice, particularly if your roommate doesn't shower and eats Doritos in bed.

When you have a roommate, you lose a fair amount of privacy. If privacy is really important to you, it's a true delay of gratification (until you graduate, get a job, and can afford to live alone).

OK- so what do I get out of all this delayed gratification?

You build wealth- which can give you peace of mind.

Here's a practical example: by changing your spending and building a savings account, you create a $1,000 emergency fund. If your car breaks down, you can pay for the repair.

NEEDS VS. WANTS

"There's a lady who's sure all that glitters is gold and she's buying a stairway to heaven"

The opening lyrics of Led Zeppelin's "Stairway to Heaven" still have great meaning for me, because the song talks about the ability (or lack of ability) to buy happiness.

There's a difference between a need (food, clothing, a roof over your head) and a want (glittering gold). You probably had a family relative lecture you on this point. I used to think that I wanted a flashy sports car. Now- not so much. Your wants change over time.

If you have something you truly want, you know that there's a tradeoff. You'll have to give something up- maybe a lot.

Think carefully before spending money on a want.

CHAPTER 5

Creating a Monthly Budget

The only reliable way to fund a savings account is to create a monthly budget and stick to your plan. That way, you'll find ways to save money and budget for a savings amount each month.

You'll save because saving money is *in your budget*.

It's time to introduce you to Sally, who you will get to know throughout the book. Here's how Sally creates her monthly budget:

- **Setting up a budget template**: Sally takes a blank piece of paper and writes her $6,000 after-tax monthly income (call it Revenue) at the top of the page. She writes down categories for Fixed Expenses, Variable Expenses, and Savings.

- **Fixed expenses**: Think about the fixed expenses you have every month. That will likely include your home mortgage, car payments, and insurance premium payments. Assume that Sally's fixed expenses add up to $4,500.

- **Variable expenses**: You now fit your variable expenses and your savings into the remaining $1,500 each month. Variable expenses are the ones you have some control over. Maybe rather than eat out three times a month, you only go twice. Sally's variable expenses total $1,200.

- **Savings account**: Your budget should include a monthly amount for savings. The first thing you do each month is pull out your budgeted savings amount and move it into a separate bank account. That way you don't spend it. As an example, 5% of monthly gross income of $6,000 would be a savings amount of $300.

Here's the budget:

Sally's Monthly Budget	
Revenue (after tax)	$6,000
Fixed expenses	$4,500
Variable expenses	$1,200
Savings	$300

There are lots of mobile apps to create and manage a monthly budget. The key is to plan your spending and review where you are a few times a month — regardless of what tool you use.

THE BENEFIT OF SAVING SOONER, RATHER THAN LATER

"I've always lived frugally and saved a lot of my income, so I don't need to work for a while"

Wow.

It was 1999, and I was talking to a co-worker, Ron, who was about 50 years old. A large insurance company we both worked for was merging with another firm, and we were both leaving the company.

I had suspected that Ron lived well below his means because I had a good idea of how much money he made. Both Ron and his wife worked, yet they lived in a neighborhood with small homes.

Ron wasn't retiring early, but he had enough money to take some time off. He told me that he and his wife had planned financially, so neither of them would need to start working immediately after leaving a job.

They planned, saved aggressively, and invested wisely.

This strategy can build wealth — even in times of market volatility.

THE IMPORTANCE OF AN EMERGENCY FUND

When you build and maintain an emergency fund, you can avoid borrowing money to pay for unexpected costs. Here are two common expenses that need to be funded:

- **Car repairs**: In most places, you need a reliable car to get to and from work. Many people started working hybrid jobs during the pandemic, and still need to go into the office a few days a week. A car repair can't be put off.

- **Insurance copayments**: Most of us pay a portion of the bill for medications, doctor visits, and other medical costs. An illness or injury is usually unplanned, and so is the cost of copayments.

When you build an emergency fund, you'll have far less anxiety when unexpected costs come up. A car repair or copayment is frustrating, but having a fund to cover the cost reduces your stress level.

I'll talk about the importance of insurance later.

The dollars you use to fund a savings/ emergency fund can't be used for some other purpose. This is a good time to talk about compounding interest- the payoff for saving money.

CHAPTER 6

Compounding Interest and the Rule of 72

Opportunity cost is defined as what you give up by choosing A rather than B.

We deal with opportunity costs all the time because we *make decisions* all the time.

- What make and model of car should I buy?
- Should I relocate to accept a work promotion?
- What career should I pursue?

Investing offers a huge opportunity.

When you invest, you can benefit from compounding interest.

THE MAGIC OF COMPOUNDING

Compounding assumes that you reinvest your earnings each year. Those earnings may be interest on a bank account, CD, or bonds. Investors also earn dividends on stock that can be reinvested in stocks or bonds.

I'll leave out gains on an investment sale for now- that complicates the issue.

By reinvesting earnings, you take advantage of the magic of compounding: the ability to earn interest on interest.

Let's use a simple example.

Let's say that you invest $100 at 5% interest. At the end of year one, you earn $5. To use compounding, you reinvest the $5 at the same interest rate. In year two, you earn 5% on **$105, or $5.25.**

You earned an extra 25 cents by compounding. The "extra" amounts you earn over time get reinvested, which generates much higher returns.

What if you keep the dollars invested longer? What's the payoff?

$100 compounding over 5 years is worth $127.63. 10 years of compounding grows the investment to $162.89.

How long would it take your money to double in value?

THE RULE OF 72

To find that answer, you can apply the Rule of 72. Take your rate of return (5%) and divide that number into 72.

- (72 / 5 = 14.4)

In 14.4 years, your money doubles.

ADDING MORE DOLLARS EACH MONTH

Many investors use paycheck withholdings to fund retirement accounts each month (I'll cover this topic later in the book). At this point, it's important to understand the compounding effect of adding dollars to that original $100 investment.

Adding $10 a month for 5 years:

- The additional dollars invested ($10 X 60 months) = $600

- Total invested dollars: Original $100 + $600 = $700

- Value after 5 years: $790.70

Start investing- at whatever pace you can. Be yourself. Any dollar amount invested will pay off for you over the long haul, and you'll feel good about what you've accomplished.

If you want to get more specific, you can use present value and future value tables to make finance decisions.

USING PRESENT VALUE TABLES

An annuity is a series of payments received over time, assuming the same dollar amounts over the same time interval. Assume that an investor will receive 10 annual payments of $36,000 and the rate of inflation is 5%.

What is that series of payments worth today?

If you Google "present value tables" you'll find tables that list the inflation rate assumptions (4%, 4.5%, etc.) on one axis and years on the other axis. The present value factor for 5% and 10 years is 7.72. The series of 10 payments is worth:

- $36,000 X 7.72 = $277,920

Note that the present value is less than ($36,000 X 10), or $360,000.

Why?

Because inflation reduces the value of the payments in future years.

Here are two examples where you can apply the present value of future payments:

- **Selling a business**: It's common for a business owner to receive a series of payments after a sale, rather than collecting the entire sale price upfront. This strategy makes it easier for the buyer to cash flow the business purchase

- **Royalties**: Royalties on music and books generate a stream of future payments

In both cases, it's important to know the present value of the future payments to assess the true value.

OK, now I'll switch over to future value tables.

FUTURE VALUE OF AN ORDINARY ANNUITY

You can use a future value calculator to find out how much you need to invest each year to reach a $1,000,000 goal. You can find great tools online.

Assume that you invest $10,500 in year one and you increase your investment by 3% each year (as your salary or other income increases). They aren't equal payments, but you still have an annuity.

Assuming an 8% annual rate of return for 25 years, you would be darn close to $1 million ($998,486.43).

CHAPTER 7

Reconciling Your Bank Account

No one likes flossing.

It's a hassle, uncomfortable — and we don't see an immediate benefit.

Sure, dentists tell us that flossing is important, but we may not see the benefits until we show up for teeth cleaning.

The same is true of reconciling your bank account.

You need to gather records, think carefully, and invest time.

However, just like flossing, reconciling your bank account each month is critical for long-term financial success.

WHY BOTHER? TWO REASONS

Reconciling your bank account helps you identify errors and possibly fraudulent transactions. Maybe your cable company overcharges you by $50. Or (worse) someone steals your debit card and charges items on your account.

The second reason is subscription fees.

IndieWire reports that: "On average, streaming households now spend $61 per month for four subscriptions to different streaming services." USA Today explains that the average monthly spending for all subscriptions is $219.

If you reconcile your bank account, you can identify subscription fees that you no longer want or need.

Convinced?

START WITH TWO DOCUMENTS

A reconciling item is a transaction that is not posted to both the check register and the bank statement. If an amount is only on *one* of the documents, the dollar amount is a reconciling item.

Here is Sally's check register (checkbook) and bank statement for May:

Check Register					Bank Statement			
May 1st	**Beginning balance**			1,200		**Beginning balance**		1,150
May 2nd	check #1106	Water bill		(50)	May 2nd	check #1106	Water bill	(50)
May 5th	debit	Cable		(200)	May 5th	debit	Cable	(200)
May 7th	check #1107	Rent		(2,500)	May 7th	check #1107	Rent	(2,500)
May 10th	debit	Uber		(30)	May 10th	debit	Uber	(30)
May 15th	direct deposit	Payroll		3,000	May 15th	direct deposit	Payroll	3,000
May 20th	check #1108	Car payment		(400)	May 22nd	debit	Bank fee	(15)
May 25th	direct deposit	Schwab stock dividend		150	May 25th	direct deposit	Bank interest on CD	40
May 30th	direct deposit	Payroll		3,000	May 30th	direct deposit	Payroll	3,000
May 31st	**Ending balance** (Balance per book)			4,170	**May 31st**	**Ending balance** (Balance per bank)		4,395

I'll say it a slightly different way, to make the point again: transactions posted to *both* the check register and the bank statement are not reconciling items. If a transaction is posted to only one document, it's a reconciling item.

The next chart is the bank reconciliation:

Bank Reconciliation				
Balance per bank statement			4,395	
Add:				
Deposits in transit				
	Schwab stock dividend		150	Deposits not posted to bank statement
Less:				
Outstanding checks				
	check #1108	Car payment	(400)	Checks not posted to bank statement
Add:				
Bank deposits not in checkbook				
	direct deposit	Bank interest on CD	40	Deposit not posted to checkbook
Less:				
Bank fees not in checkbook				
	debit	Bank fee	(15)	Debit not posted to checkbook
Equals:				
Adjusted cash balance			4,170	

The $4,170 adjusted cash balance fully accounts for all transactions in the check register (checkbook) and the bank statement.

Final note: Complete a bank reconciliation as soon as the bank statement is available. The faster you find errors and fraudulent transactions, the better. If you put off bank reconciliations, you may be managing your finances with an incorrect bank balance.

CHAPTER 8

How To Recover from a Financial Setback

"Experience is what you get when you don't get what you want."

That quote is attributed to Randy Pausch. I highly recommend his TED Talk that is referred to as The Last Lecture. Pausch, a college professor, gave the talk when he was dying of cancer.

I've always said that resilience is the number one personal trait that people need to have. My father passed away in March of 2019, and his headstone has the phrase "Be Resilient".

My hope for my three kids is that they can pick themselves up off the deck when they are floored by life. They range in age from 33 to 24 and have demonstrated resilience, which gives me peace of mind.

In the Spring of 2016, I had a financial punch to the face. If you've faced (or are facing) a financial setback, I hope these thoughts help you.

WHAT HAPPENED

I'm self-employed as an author, writer and video producer. I seek out work by making pitches and responding to incoming requests. Somehow, the stars aligned, and I got burned by doing a lot of work with poor clients. Here are some examples of what clients said- and what they *meant*:

- "I expect perfect grammar": That means that I don't value people and that my demands are completely unreasonable.

- "We need a ton of work from you": This means that they haven't carefully thought about the project and what quality work is required to complete it.

- "I'm starting an online publication." This person had no experience with anything close to starting or running a publication.

Not surprisingly, I did a lot of work for these types of people and either got paid late- or not at all. I lost thousands of dollars in income, which created a financial setback.

OK — enough whining. Let's all learn from this situation.

STEP ONE: MOVE TOWARD THE PROBLEM

I've been married for 37 years, and it's taken.... well, about 37 years...to realize that I must face problems head-on with my wife. Invariably, when I confront a problem, it's not nearly so dire.

In this case, I sat down with my wife, Patty. I told her how much revenue I had lost, and we planned our finances (as best we could) to cash flow ourselves without the income that was lost.

Now, that's not easy for a couple, because one person has to give their partner bad news. Once the bad news is digested, the couple needs to put together a plan- and the plan needs to be in place quickly, to avoid creating bigger financial problems.

This step is tough- but necessary.

STEP TWO: CREATE A BUDGET (IF YOU HAVEN'T ALREADY)

Chapter 5 explains how to create a monthly budget and the benefits of sticking to a budget. Once the smoke clears from a financial setback, take another look at this issue.

If you have a budget, reassess your monthly spending and create a plan to fix the hole created by the financial setback. That may mean one or more of these steps:

- **Cutting expenses**: You may need to cut back on discretionary spending in your monthly budget. Maybe you dine out less for a few months, or you can reduce the cost of a vacation.
- **Consolidation loan:** You may able to consolidate your credit card and student loan debts into one loan with

a lower interest rate. Say, for example, that you pay off debts with an average rate of 12% and replace them with a single loan at a 9% rate. Good for you- the rate is lower. However, if you need to extend the maturity date to get a lower monthly payment, the total interest you pay over the life of the loan may be higher at 9%.

- **Increase your income:** If you generate income on your own, you can find new business to replace the income you lost. That will take time- and you won't be able to recoup that lost income for some time. You'll probably need to cut expenses or renegotiate debts in the short term until the new business is billed.

Take a long look at each of these strategies.

STEP 3: OPTIONS YOU SHOULD AVOID

A loss of income can be emotional, and it can be difficult to keep things in perspective. There are some actions to avoid:

- **Doubt your abilities:** Winston Churchill is quoted as saying: "Success is going from failure to failure without a loss of enthusiasm." Everyone tries and fails- so don't be too hard on yourself. Don't doubt your abilities.

- **High-interest loans:** Taking out a high-interest loan should only be a last resort- if you really can't cash flow any other way.

- **New credit cards**: Same thing here. Many people take out a credit card as a short-term fix, and then don't pay it off. The best step is to avoid new credit cards altogether.

NOW YOU'RE READY

There's one bright spot when you have to address a financial setback: The next time it happens (and it will), you'll be prepared. You'll react with less emotion, and you can fix the problem faster. Build a savings balance over time, so that you're prepared for the unexpected the next time it rolls around.

Now, I'll shift into a discussion of investment options.

CHAPTER 9

Understanding Common Stocks

I drink two sodas each day, which concerns my wife.

She sends me articles with titles like: "10 Reasons Why Soda Is Killing You".

Subtle...

Many investors own common stock, and I'll explain the different types of accounts that are used to own stock later. For now, I'll explain the basics of common stock using PepsiCo as an example.

HOW COMPANIES RAISE MONEY TO OPERATE

There are two basic ways that a company can raise money to run a business: issue debt or sell stock to the public. The money raised is referred to as capital. Most of the investments you'll consider are some combination of stocks and bonds.

Years ago, PepsiCo issued common stock to the public for the first time. If Sally purchases common stock, she becomes an owner (a shareholder) of PepsiCo.

SHAREHOLDER RIGHTS

Sally has some rights as a shareholder:

- **Voting rights**: Shareholders vote on major business decisions, such as electing the board of directors or approving a merger with another company. PepsiCo sends Sally documentation that allows her to vote her shares at the annual meeting. She doesn't need to be present to vote.

- **Cash dividends**: Dividends are a share of company profits (earnings), and PepsiCo may pay a portion of profits as a cash dividend. A company does not have to pay a dividend, and many firms retain profits for use in the business.

- **Stock dividend**: A company may reward you by issuing more shares of stock to existing shareholders. For example, you might receive 1 share of stock for every 10 shares you own. More on stock dividends later in the book.

- **Stock sale**: You have the right to sell your common stock and you can sell stock on most business days. Shareholders can profit by selling stock for gain.

If you hold common stock for years, you can earn either cash dividends, stock dividends, or both over those years. Dividends allow you to profit, even if the stock price stays the same or declines.

STOCK AND COMPANY LIQUIDATIONS

Common stock owners are last in line to receive assets if a company liquidates.

It's unusual, but a concept you need to know.

If a company is forced to sell its assets, who gets the assets?

- **Secured creditors**: Creditors who own an interest in a particular company asset are paid first. If a bank has a mortgage on the company headquarters, they have the right to the sales proceeds when the building is sold.

- **Bondholders**: I'll explain bonds in an upcoming chapter. A corporate bond may be backed by specific assets (building, equipment), or an unsecured bond backed by the company's "ability to pay". Credit card debts are usually unsecured loans, for example.

- **Common stockholders**: If you own common stock, you are last in line to receive assets if the company liquidates.

Again, this situation is unusual, but companies do go bankrupt. A large, profitable business like PepsiCo isn't much of a risk, but less profitable companies might be.

PROOF OF OWNERSHIP

When you buy stock, what's your proof of ownership?

Years ago, most stock certificates were issued in physical form. Today, nearly all stock certificates are in book entry form (a computerized certificate). A registrar (an independent third party) is responsible for tracking the ownership of each common stock share and they issue stock certificates.

Now that you understand the basics, how are stocks traded?

CHAPTER 10

How Stocks Are Traded

Who is Roaring Kitty?

He had his second 15 minutes of fame…

Roaring Kitty is Keith Gill, a popular influencer on Reddit who gained fame by recommending GameStop stock during the meme stock trading frenzy. Dumb Money is a good (not great) movie that dramatizes meme stock trading in recent years.

On June 12, 2024, CNBC reported that Gill owned 5 million shares of GameStop common stock and a huge position in GameStop stock options.

In late June of '24, the GameStop stock price had huge volatility as people speculated on the stock price. This is a great way to introduce how stocks trade. Ask this question:

"If I sell my GameStop shares, is there a willing buyer? What price will they pay me for my shares?"

BID PRICE, ASK PRICE, AND THE SPREAD

Stock buyers pay the ask price and sellers receive the bid price.

Let's say that you own IBM common stock — a publicly traded stock. That means that the securities are registered with the SEC and that the stock trades on an exchange.

Assume the NASDAQ exchange reports that IBM is trading at around $150 per share.

Stocks trade with a bid and ask price. The bid is what you can currently sell the stock for, and the ask is the price you would pay to buy the stock. The difference between the bid and ask prices is the spread.

The spread can be thought of as the profit earned by anyone making a market in the stock. It's as if you put the stock in your shop's display window at the ask price (say $150). If someone brings the stock into your shop and wants to sell it, they would receive the bid price (say $149.50). With improvements in technology, the spread on a large stock like IBM is very small.

THE MOVIE TICKET LINE: HOW A BID PRICE IS DETERMINED

So, what is stock trading? If you want to sell your IBM stock, you'll receive the bid price. We've experienced periods of huge stock price volatility in recent years, and what that means to you is that the bid price can decline rapidly in a volatile market. That price you receive for your shares may be less (maybe much less) than you anticipated.

Think about a line at a movie theatre. You notice 5 people in line for tickets as you pull up to the theatre. Since the line isn't long, you decide to park first, rather than let your spouse out to grab a place in line.

After you park and head for the ticket window, there are 20 people in line.

The same thing can happen when you want to sell your stock. With stocks, you have a certain number of people willing to buy stock (possibly your stock) at a given price. Say, for instance, that there are currently 50,000 shares at the $149.50 bid price. Those 50,000 shares are similar to a number of people in line at the movie theatre.

You get the bid price, which could be *any* price...

Assume that bad news comes out on IBM. Well, those buyers at $149.50 may decide against buying IBM at that price. Say, for instance, that 40,000 of those potential buyers go away. They decide they'd only buy at $145.

You have a market maker who is dealing with buyers and sellers- each of whom may buy or sell a different number of shares. Since 40,000 shares worth of the buyers at $149.50 went away, only 10,000 shares are sold at $149.50. If you weren't toward the front of line, you won't receive $149.50 — you'll sell at a lower price.

As more buyers cut the price they are willing to pay for your IBM stock, the bid price declines. Your stock, sadly, is "on sale".

THE GAMESTOP TRADING RISK

GameStop (and other meme) stocks illustrate the bid and ask system in the extreme. During the last GameStop trading frenzy, people who put in sell orders had sell trades get executed (orders filled) at prices far below the bid price when the order was placed.

Why?

The stock price declined sharply- and as buying interest evaporated, the bid price crashed.

THE LESSON

Less volatile stocks have smaller fluctuations in the bid and ask prices. The sale price you receive or the purchase price you pay may not change much from the current bid and ask prices.

When you place buy or sell orders for volatile stocks, prices can change sharply.

That's a discussion about the risks of buying stock. Let's move on a talk about the potential rewards.

CHAPTER 11

Common Stocks Returns

Wait- they closed the drive-thru window?

I had to deposit a check, so I drove by a Bank of America branch. I rarely if ever get client checks, and I hadn't visited a bank in over a year.

I waited in line while one person got 7 different rolls of coins, and a second person tried to deposit a 5-year-old third-party check. OK- I made up the part about the check, but I waited nearly 10 minutes.

The point? I had expectations that the bank could quickly handle my deposit so I could move on with my day.

The same is true of most investor's beliefs about the returns they can earn on stock:

THREE TYPES OF RETURNS

Generally speaking, there are three ways to earn a return on a stock.

- **Price appreciation**: You profit from selling the stock for more than you paid

- **Cash dividend**: The company pays you a cash dividend, which is a share of company earnings

- **Stock dividend**: You receive a dividend in the form of additional stock, and you can benefit from price appreciation and/or a cash dividend on the new shares

To profit from the stock market over time, you must do something completely counterintuitive.

WHEN YOU SENSE DANGER, *DON'T* RUN

The U.S. stock market has been an effective tool for investors to generate profits for decades — if you're willing to be patient and accept volatility.

Notice how I added that "disclaimer" about patience and volatility? When it comes to investing, most people aren't willing to accept these two realities.

Dire Straits had a big hit with a song called: "Money For Nothing" in the 80s — and investing in the stock market is not a money-for-nothing proposition. If you're willing to live with the short-term risk and volatility, the stock market can generate earnings over the long term.

HOW LONG IS THE "LONG TERM"?

Long term is from 1928 until today.

One tool to measure how the stock market has performed is the Standard and Poor's 500 index (S&P 500). This is an index of 500 frequently traded stocks in the US markets. The S&P 500 index includes many names you've heard of — think Microsoft and Proctor & Gamble.

The idea here is that the S&P 500 index behaves in a way that reflects the market as a whole. It's an indicator of where all stocks may be headed.

So how has this index performed over time? Seeking Alpha provides a great list that shows the S&P 500's total return from 1928 to 2015. Total return assumes that capital gains (selling the stock for a gain) and dividends earned are reinvested.

As Seeking Alpha points out: "Over 88 years, the S&P 500 went up 64 years and went down 24 years.... The worst return was -43.84% in 1931. The best return was 52.56% in 1954."

Now, that may strike you as encouraging or terrifying. I get it.

Rather than looking at year-to-year, consider the average return over time.

Investopedia explains that "The average annualized return since its (S&P 500's) inception in 1928 through

Dec. 31, 2023, is 9.90%. The average annualized return since adopting 500 stocks into the index in 1957 through Dec. 31, 2023, is 10.26%."

A 10% return allows you to double your money every 7.2 years. As discussed in chapter 6, Take your rate of return (10%) and divide that number into 72.

- (72 / 10 = 7.2)

Imagine how much wealth you can accumulate over 20 or 30 years...

THE LESSON

Be a realist- don't expect more than the S&P 500 average return over time. The ups and downs from one year to the next can be jarring- but stay focused on the average return over 10 years, 20 years- whatever your investing time horizon is.

Past performance is no guarantee of future returns. Discuss risks and returns with an investment advisor.

Many investors own both stocks and bonds. I'll review bonds next.

CHAPTER 12

Understanding Bond Investing

Based on what I see on social media, hundreds of people are "crushing life goals".

The typical comments look like this: "I sold my startup business for an 8-figure exit price, lost 50 pounds, went to Burning Man, and live with my soulmate."

You're asked to read a thread, attend a course, or join the online community to find out how *you too* can crush life.

'Trouble is that most people aren't crushing life. We all struggle, make mistakes, and learn from the experience. This is true for most investors.

You read earlier that companies raise money to operate the business in two ways: issue stock or issue bonds. I'll assume that Sally (our investor) can invest using stocks, bonds, or both.

In Chapters 9, 10, and 11, I introduced the basics of common stock investing. Now let's move to bond investing.

BOND BASICS

Corporations, municipalities (states, cities), and the federal government can issue bonds. Here are some bond investing terms:

- **Issuer**: Assume that IBM (the issuer) issues a corporate bond

- **Face amount (par amount)**: The *amount* that IBM must repay the bondholder when the bond matures. This dollar amount is also referred to as the principal amount

- **Maturity date:** The *date* that IBM must repay the bondholder

- **Coupon rate**: The interest rate used to calculate interest payments

- **Bond rating**: A letter rating that ranks the creditworthiness of the issuer. In other words, how likely is it that IBM will pay all interest and principal payments on time?

Standard and Poor's (S&P) rates bonds from AAA (highest) to D (lowest). Investment-grade bonds are rated from AAA down to BBB, and most investment advisors only recommend investment-grade bonds.

BOND PRICES AND BOND YIELDS

Bonds trade in the marketplace, just like stocks, and the price of a bond can change.

Assume that IBM issues an AA-rated $5,000 6% 10-year corporate bond at par, or $5,000. Each year the investor earns 6% on $5,000, or $300, and that $300 payment never changes for the 10 years the bond is outstanding.

Now, assume that interest rates increase. Economists will tell you that when more buyers attempt to buy the same amount of goods, prices go up, causing inflation. Inflation can also lead to higher interest rates.

If comparable corporate bonds (same AA credit rating) can be issued at 8%, the 6% IBM bond will decline in value.

Why?

Because investors can buy a new bond issue at 8%. As a result, the $5,000 IBM 6% bond might be worth only $4,800.

THE BOND'S TOTAL RETURN

So, why would someone buy the 6% bond if new bonds of similar quality are issued at 8%?

If the buyer can pay a discount, the 6% purchase might make sense.

A bond's total return (also called yield to maturity) is the interest income plus any gain or loss on the bond when it matures. If an investor buys the $5,000 IBM 6% bond for $4,800 the total return is:

Annual interest: $300 in annual interest payments, *plus*

Gain on bond: The difference between the $4,800 cost and the $5,000 received at maturity is a $200 gain.

When you speak with an investment advisor about bonds, ask about the bond's total return.

Bonds may offer more predictability than stocks. The IBM bondholder can hold the corporate bond until maturity and know the interest and principal amounts that will be paid (assuming that IBM maintains a good credit rating).

Rather than buying individual stocks and bonds, many investors purchase mutual funds that contain stocks and bonds.

CHAPTER 13

Mutual Fund Investing Options

I think my dog groomer is making a fortune.

The building is less than 1,000 square feet and always busy. I've been taking dogs to this groomer for 20 years, and I've never seen a slow day.

I think I know why.

Customers know what they're getting. The staff is very clear about what they can do and (more importantly) what they *can't do*. If you think your dog will compete in the Westminster Dog Show, you probably need to take Princess Caroline somewhere else.

Clarity. It's something that investors don't always have.

Did you hear these comments during tax season?

"You need to open a retirement account to take the deduction on your tax return."

"Do you have a 1099-DIV for the dividend you were paid on the IBM stock?"

Completing your tax return is tough enough- then tax preparers and investment advisors throw in these other questions.

Mutual funds can be particularly confusing.

What investments are in my mutual fund? Do I have to pay taxes each year? If I sell the fund, what is the tax impact?

I'll use the Box, the Bag, and the Wrapper Analogy to clear up these issues.

YOUR AMAZON SHIPMENT

Ok, let's assume that you get a box from Amazon. Inside the box are 10 bags, and each bag contains individually wrapped pieces of candy.

Got it?

THE BOX:
THE TYPE OF INVESTMENT ACCOUNT

The box is the type of brokerage account you use to purchase the mutual fund. Generally speaking, there are two types of accounts:

- **Taxable account**: The interest on bonds, dividends on stock, and capital gains or losses are reported on your tax return each year.

- **Retirement account**: The most common retirement account is a 401(k) account through your employer, and you can set up other types of retirement accounts if you're self-employed. The tax impact of interest, dividends, and capital gains and losses is deferred. There is no tax impact until you withdraw funds at retirement.

401(k) retirement accounts may include contributions from your employer that are not taxed until retirement. If your company contributes an additional $1,000 to your 401(k) plan, that money grows tax deferred. Since taxes are delayed until you take money out at retirement, you accumulate wealth faster.

THE BAG:
THE MUTUAL FUND

Inside the box (the account) may be one or more mutual fund investments. For example, Washington Mutual is a fund that invests in U.S. equities (common stock).

To diversify investment risk, your account may include different types of mutual funds, including stock funds, bond funds, and balanced funds (that invest in both stocks and bonds).

THE WRAPPERS:
THE FUND INVESTMENTS

A bag (mutual fund) may own dozens — or hundreds — of individual stocks and bonds (candy wrappers). Washington Mutual owns dozens of stocks in a variety of industries. As of this writing, the fund owns shares in 188 different stocks.

CLEARING UP TAX CONFUSION

If your box is a taxable account, you can expect to receive tax documents from the mutual fund that report interest income, dividend income, and possibly capital gains and losses each year. If the box is a retirement account, the tax impact is deferred until you sell the investment.

If your mutual fund buys and sells stocks in a taxable account, you'll pay taxes on interest income, dividend income, and capital gains each year. Stock or bond sales in a retirement plan do not impact your taxes until you withdraw funds.

Keep this example in mind as you start to invest.

I'll dig a little deeper into retirement plans next.

CHAPTER 14

Understanding Retirement Plans

Is every flat surface now a pickleball court?

Basketball courts, tennis courts, backyards — the sport is everywhere.

Most annoying is all the old people showing up at my gym to play pickleball. They don't attend my classes- but they walk slowly. It's sort of like Night of the Living Dead carrying pickleball equipment.

Pickleball is everywhere, just like financial service ads for retirement plans. In fact, Morgan Stanley and JP Morgan are marketing retirement plans to the Night of the Living Dead demographic...

Back in Chapter 5, Sally created a monthly budget that included savings of $300 per month. Assume that Sally has accumulated $1,000 in savings for an emergency fund, and she now wants to invest that $300 each month moving forward.

A retirement plan allows Sally to accumulate investment earnings much faster than investing in a taxable account. She decides to use her employer's 401(k) retirement plan.

RETIREMENT PLAN BENEFITS

Most 401(k) plans allow you to invest pretax dollars into a retirement plan that's provided through your job. When Sally invests $300 each month in the company's 401(k) plan, the entire $300 is invested.

The $300 investment — and all of the earnings — aren't taxed until she takes money out of the plan at retirement.

If Sally didn't use the company plan, she'd pay taxes on the $300 *before investing*. So, not as much money would be invested.

So how much more gets invested using a 401(k) plan?

MORE DOLLARS INVESTED

Here is Sally's salary, the tax on the salary, and her after-tax income:

Annual salary	$96,000
Tax (25%)	$24,000
After-tax annual income	$72,000

Sally's monthly after-tax income in Chapter 5 is $6,000, or annual income of ($6,000 X 12), or $72,000.

If Sally invests in the 401(k) plan, the entire $300 is invested. If she invests outside of a retirement plan, the dollars invested total ($300 X 75%), or $225. $75 goes to pay taxes.

Over 20 to 30 years, that extra $75 investment each month can make a huge difference in Sally's total return.

The dollars invested directly in the 401(k) account also reduce Sally's taxable income- but that's a story of another day. For now, I'll keep the focus on her investment.

HOW A RETIREMENT PLAN MATCH BENEFITS YOU

A retirement plan match refers to the additional pre-tax dollars an employer will invest in your retirement plan, based on the amount you personally invest.

Let's say that Sally can receive an extra 5% match on her 401(k) contributions. If you don't invest in your 401(k) and get the company matching dollars, you're leaving money on the table. That extra 5% adds up over time.

The employer 401(k) match increases Sally's monthly contribution from $300 to $315.

Find out if your employer offers a retirement plan. Speak with an investment advisor about retirement plan details.

CHAPTER 15

Selecting an Investment Advisor

When the political season heats up, the media will use these phrases constantly:

"Revving up the base"

"It's all about turnout"

"Engaged voters"

If you're playing political bingo, your card must include these phrases.

The same is true with ads for investment advisors. All the ads use phrases like:

"Trusted advisor"

"Helping you meet your goals"

"Tailored to fit your needs"

I can make a strong case that everyone should work with an investment advisor.

Why?

None of us make good decisions when we're under stress. When we're anxious or "under the gun", we may not think clearly.

These are the types of situations that may lead to a bad decision. When you make an investment decision, you benefit from speaking with a financial professional.

A 2015 article in the Wall Street Journal discusses research from Vanguard, a large mutual fund company. Vanguard's study found:

"Brokers and advisors perform a vital service by keeping clients invested for the long term. The decision to stay invested during times of market stress swamps all other factors affecting retirement savings".

So, here's what you need to know to select an investment advisor.

I UNDERSTAND FINANCE — DO I NEED AN ADVISOR?

Yes — I think you do.

I have a background in finance (let's hope so- I write about finance for clients). A person like me might say: "I've got this covered on my own- why work with a financial advisor?"

What if you have a medical emergency?

I had emergency surgery in 2021 and was in the hospital for a week. I was in no condition to make financial decisions for another 10 days after getting home.

I think everyone needs an advisor- even people who work in finance.

YEARS OF EXPERIENCE

OK, this sounds obvious- but there's a specific reason why experience is particularly important.

Has the advisor worked with clients during market downturns?

Consider what's happened in the past 25 years:

To explain, consider Investopedia's data on the Standard and Poor's (S&P) 500 annual returns for the last 25 years. These returns assume that the investor reinvested any cash dividend payments:

- **2008 Financial Crisis**: 36.55% decline

- **Dot Com Financial Crisis**: 11.85% decline in 2001, 21.97% decline in 2002

I want an advisor who helped clients navigate one (or both) of these market declines.

The guidance may have sounded like this:

"We've had market downturns like this before. You still own quality stocks and bonds issued by companies that have been profitable over the long term. Based on 80-plus years of market history, prices will eventually go back up. There's no reason to sell anything."

Now, every advisor must add: "Past performance does not guarantee future performance."

I get it.

You need an advisor who has "survived" a big market downturn by providing wise counsel to customers. If the advisor didn't do an effective job during a downturn, he or she wouldn't have any clients.

RESPONSIVE TO CUSTOMERS

Can you get your advisor on the phone when you have a question?

Many large financial firms have decided to focus on clients with the highest net worth. To free up each advisor's time to service the "big fish" customers, smaller accounts are given an 800 number to call.

Well, what if you're not a big fish?

Life events happen. A parent passes away and a child must unravel the parent's investment accounts. You're closing on a home loan and need to move funds for closing costs (my daughter had this issue).

Customer service people are nice and well-meaning but don't know you personally.

Can they solve your problem?

Ask the advisor if you can get them on the phone- or someone in the office that knows you. If they work for a large financial service company (I won't name the specific firms), the answer may be no.

THE BEST WAY TO FIND AN ADVISOR

The best way- hands down- is to ask friends for a referral.

It's an important decision that is similar to finding a doctor or an attorney. Rely on people you know and trust to refer you to the right advisor.

CHAPTER 16

Reviewing Common Investor Mistakes

I'm trapped by two-factor authorization (2FA).

It seems like every app and tool I log into now requires that extra code to log in. I don't know how much time 2FA requires, but it's taking years off my life.

It's a hassle, but 2FA is necessary to protect data. Turning it off would be a mistake.

Big swings in stock prices may have you wondering if you've made some huge mistakes, and that's normal when investing tensions are running high. To assess if you're on track, here's my list of the most common mistakes investors make.

FORGETTING YOUR INVESTING GOAL (OR NOT HAVING ONE AT ALL)

For starters, go back to the reason you started investing in the first place. Specifically, how much money were you trying to accumulate, and for what purpose? How long were you planning to invest?

Let's assume, for example, that you're investing now in a 401(k) retirement account and 25 years from retirement. You're willing to take a moderate amount of risk. If your portfolio is up or down 10% in one year, you can live with it. A 25% change, however, makes your palms sweaty.

You invested in mutual funds, with 70% in stock and 30% in bonds.

That's the plan- and that's where you start.

UNREALISTIC EXPECTATIONS

Let's go back to 2018.

As of 1/22/18, the Dow Jones Industrial Average (DJIA) closed at 26,214.60, up 32.4% in the prior 12 months. The DJIA is an index of 30 large corporate stocks.

A broader index, the Standard and Poor's (S&P) 500, closed at 2,832.97 on 1/22, and this is an index of 500 large stocks- a bigger basket of stocks. The S&P 500 was up 24.7% over the prior 12 months.

Crazy, record-setting performance... and it's stressful to consider the fact that every bull market ends. Expecting a 25%-plus annual return is simply not realistic.

It may seem like everyone around you is getting rich — but high returns may come at a price

The people who are really killing it in the markets are taking more risk (Bitcoin, anyone?). They either:

- Have a large percentage of their total portfolios in stock (vs. bond or cash), and/or

- They're buying riskier stocks that have an inconsistent history of earnings and sales.

You need to keep your head and realize:

- Your goals haven't changed

- Bull markets, historically, come to an end at some point

- When (not if) the bull market ends, you may incur some losses in the short term

But you can get through it.

SO, WHAT IS A NORMAL RETURN?

So, what's a "normal return" on stocks, if such a number exists?

Seeking Alpha says 11%, and other stats suggest 8-10% over a 70 to 80 year period. The point is that 24-32% isn't normal.

Accept the fact that, over the long run, you're not going to earn more than the historical "normal" return.

RISK ASSESSMENT

Most investors do not **honestly** assess risk tolerance. Note that word- honestly. To assess your risk tolerance, ask yourself this question: If your portfolio's value went up or down 10% in one year, is that something you could live with? How about 20%?

You get the idea.

Use that knowledge to select your investments. If you want a stock mutual fund with moderate risk, read the fund's investment objective and check the fund's historical performance. Specifically, check out the fund's beta, which measures a fund's volatility in comparison with the broad stock market, such as the S&P 500.

SUCCEEDING ONCE IS RANDOM

Ask that guy who just hit 21 playing his first hand of blackjack at a casino. He may think he's a genius, but the law of large numbers removes randomness. Over time, the blackjack player's results will shift back to a normal level. In the same way, great investors succeed over the long term- when returns are no longer random.

FINAL THOUGHTS

- Have an investment plan, and avoid emotional decisions (particularly sell decisions)

- Invest in companies that consistently make money- and hold those stocks

- Timing the market (i.e. buying or selling at precisely the right time) doesn't work over the long haul, so don't try it

- Diversify your portfolio into stocks and bonds that perform differently in up and down markets. That approach will help you average out your total returns over time.

Discuss these concepts with a financial advisor.

Asset allocation models are a great tool for investors- I'll explain that topic next.

CHAPTER 17

Asset Allocation Models

I don't like roller coasters.

In fact, I don't care for any type of amusement ride.

About 10 years ago, we took our kids to our community's annual carnival, and I rode The Scrambler. Dad had to go home because he was dizzy...

No one likes sharp declines in the stock market from year to year. In Chapter 11, I used Seeking Alpha's data on the history of the stock market.

"Over 88 years, the S&P 500 went up 64 years and went down 24 years.... The worst return was -43.84% in 1931. The best return was 52.56% in 1954."

Now, THAT'S a roller coaster.

But don't panic. Instead, focus on the long-term average rate of returns for stocks, which I discussed earlier. Over time, 8-10% is probably realistic.

Edward Jones has told investors for years that: "Time in the market is more important than *timing* the market."

Over time, the market has recovered. That has to be true, or the average return over time would be negative- not positive.

HOW TO MEASURE STOCK VOLATILITY

Beta is a term that measures volatility in the price of an investment and beta is a useful tool for investors to understand risk.

Assume, for example, that you're buying stock in IBM, a large company. Analysts will measure the volatility of IBM's common stock by comparing the stock price change to the performance of an index. If the S&P 500 is used, this index is referred to as the benchmark for the beta calculation.

Here's how beta works:

- A beta of 1 means that IBM stock moves up and down in perfect correlation with the index. If the S&P 500 index goes up 7%, so does the IBM stock.

- Betas of <u>less than 1</u> mean that the stock is *less volatile* than the index.

- A beta of <u>more than 1</u> indicates that the stock is *more volatile*.

If you prefer less fluctuation, choose a low-beta stock. Investors who want to take more risk look for high-beta stocks.

Why not group investments by type, rather than evaluate one investment at a time?

A BETTER WAY: ASSET ALLOCATION MODELS

Nearly every financial advisory firm offers a model investment portfolio. It's an ideal blend of stock, bonds, and other investments, based on your age, risk tolerance, and investment goals. For this discussion, I'll focus on only stocks and bonds.

Here are three common asset allocation models:

- **Income portfolio:** 70% to 100% in bonds. The primary goal is to generate dividends on stocks and interest payments on bonds. If the stock prices increase over time, even better.

- **Growth portfolio:** 70% to 100% in stocks. The primary goal is to produce capital gains by selling stocks at a profit. The portfolio will also generate dividends on stocks and interest payments on bonds, but that's a secondary objective.

- **Balanced portfolio:** 40% to 60% in stocks. As the name implies, the goal is both income and growth in some combination.

Ask an investment advisor which portfolio is right for you.

WHY TIME IS AN IMPORTANT FACTOR

Keep in mind that younger people can afford to take more risk because the investor has more years to recover from stock market losses. A 25-year-old may invest a bigger percentage of the portfolio in stocks than a 60-year-old.

Why?

If the stock portfolio declines in value, the 25-year-old has more years to wait for a market recovery. A 60-year-old who is retiring in 5 years has less time to make up for losses.

This is true whether IBM is sold at a loss, or if the stock is held by the investor during a market decline. Younger investors have more time.

In Chapter 13, I explained that Sally (our investor) is investing $315 a month into her employer's 401(k) retirement plan. Sally is 35 years old and decides to use a growth portfolio with 70% in stocks and 30% in bonds.

CHAPTER 18

Why Earnings Per Share Is Important

A heavy-set man with a limp was trying to drag a heavy bag off the baggage carousel.

He started to lose his balance, so I grabbed the suitcase and pulled it off for him.

Now I'm no hero, but it did remind me of something.

There are dozens of ways that financial analysts evaluate stocks. If you watch the media, you may feel bombarded by investment terms. It's a lot like watching how fast luggage moves on the baggage carousel.

It can feel overwhelming.

It's important to leave much of the analysis to an investment advisor, which is a point I've made throughout the book.

However, every investor should understand the concept of earnings per share. This concept is the basis for many types of stock valuation. Simply put, firms that consistently generate earnings are seen as more valuable than businesses that aren't profitable yearly.

EARNINGS PER SHARE: THE PLAY-DOH ANALOGY

Did you have a Play-Doh machine as a kid?

You put the dough in the toy, turn the handle, and the dough comes out in different shapes on the other end.

That's like generating company earnings. In our discussion, earnings, net income, and profit mean the same thing. Here's how the machine works:

- The dough you put in is the material and labor costs to make a product or service
- Turning the handle means creating the product or service
- The dough that comes out is the profit on the sale

Businesses "turn the crank" on the Play-Doh machine every month to produce profits.

EARNINGS PER SHARE FORMULA

Earnings per share (EPS) is defined as:

(Net income available to common stock) / (average shares of common stock outstanding).

In other words, how much did the company earn on each share of common stock?

Not all net income may be available for common shareholders. Firms that issue preferred stock may set aside net income to pay a preferred dividend before a common stock dividend (hence the term "preferred" stock).

Let's assume that Premier Manufacturing earns $5,000,000 and that the average number of common stock shares outstanding is 2,000,000 shares.

EPS is ($5,000,000 / 2,000,000 shares), or $2.50 per share.

If there are more common stock shares outstanding, the earnings per share will be lower. That's because you're "spreading" the same amount of profit ($5,000,000) over more shares of stock.

So, is $2.50 a good, bad, or average return?

The answer is found in the earnings yield:

Earnings yield = (Earnings per share) / (Market price of common stock per share)

If Premier's common stock price is $60 per share, the earnings yield is:

($2.50 earnings per share) / ($60 market price), or 4.2% (with rounding).

You want a high earnings yield compared to the average yield for similar stocks.

Here's what I mean.

Assume that a money manager is analyzing five stocks in the food industry. All five companies grow earnings at about 5% per year. The stock with the highest earnings yield is more attractive because the earnings are highest when compared to the stock's market price.

In other words, you get more earnings for each dollar of market price.

Here's the challenge of investing when markets are near an all-time high: When the price you pay for a stock is higher, the earnings yield is lower. Essentially, you're paying a higher amount for each dollar of earnings.

Keep this discussion in mind when you hear the term earnings per share.

Now, I'll dive into the ways you can profit from owning stock.

CHAPTER 19

CrowdStrike, Stock Dividends, and Shareholder Returns

I guess I was lucky to be on Southwest...

CrowdStrike is a cybersecurity technology company. Many large businesses rely on CrowdStrike to protect data from cyber threats.

In July of 2024 a Microsoft software update was mishandled by CrowdStrike. As a result, multiple airlines had to cancel thousands of flights. Delta claimed that the outage cost the business $500 million.

I showed up at the airport to fly Southwest home from vacation. The airport was half empty.

How do travelers value an airline?

Do they reliably get me where I want to go at a reasonable price? You can imagine the angry customers contacting Delta, American, and other airlines during the outage.

Financial advisors use metrics to measure the value of investments.

MEASURING THE VALUE OF A CASH DIVIDEND

Dividend yield reports the rate of return on a dividend, based on the current market price of the stock:

Dividend yield = (Annual dividend per share) / (Market price of common stock per share)

In this example, Premier Manufacturing pays a $1.25 dividend when the stock price is $60 per share. The dividend yield is ($1.25 annual dividend) / ($60 market price), or 2.1% (with rounding). Think about it this way: If an investor purchases Premier at $60 per share, they are "buying" a 2.1% dividend return.

The dividend payout ratio points out the percentage of company earnings paid as a dividend:

Dividend payout ratio = (Common stock dividend) / (Earnings available to common shareholder)

If Premier's earnings per share (EPS) is $2.50, the dividend payout ratio is ($1.25 dividend) / ($2.50 EPS), of 50%.

COMPUTE SHAREHOLDER RETURN ON A STOCK

Financial advisors use this formula to measure shareholder returns:

(Increase in common stock price + Annual dividend per share) / (beginning common stock price for the period)

To calculate the shareholder return, assume the following:

- Premier's stock price increases $2 per share in a year

- The stock pays a $1.25 dividend

- The beginning stock price for the period is $60 per share

The annual shareholder return is:

($2 increase in common stock price + $1.25 annual dividend per share) / ($60 beginning common stock price) = ($3.25 / $60), or 5.4%

But there's a third benefit from owning stock that's not included in the formula: a stock dividend

EVALUATING STOCK DIVIDENDS

Assume that Premier pays a 10% stock dividend, and that our investor Sally owns 100 shares. Sally received (100 shares X 10%), or 10 more shares.

That's 10 more shares that can increase in price, earn a dividend — or both.

In some cases, bonds can be converted into common stock.

CHAPTER 20

Turkish Silver Medalist, Preferred Stock and Convertible Securities

Olympic competitors use the best equipment.

Did you happen to see the 2024 Turkish silver medalist in pistol shooting?

Stood with his normal glasses on and a hand in his pocket. No special goggles on other equipment. He came in second.

To succeed as an investor, sometimes you just need to learn the basics. The basics include preferred stock and convertible securities.

WHAT IS PREFERRED STOCK?

The word "preferred" means "better", and that's true of preferred stock. Preferred stock is better than common stock for two reasons:

- **Dividends:** If the company pays a dividend out of earnings, preferred shareholders receive their dividends before common shareholders. If there's not enough money to pay the common stock dividend, only the preferred stock dividend is paid.

- **Claim on Assets:** If the company liquidates, preferred shareholders have a claim on assets that's ahead of common stockholders. Common shares are last in line to make a claim on assets.

Investors may own convertible preferred stock or convertible bonds.

WHAT ARE CONVERTIBLE SECURITIES?

Convertible preferred shareholders have the right (at some point) to convert their preferred shares into common stock. The shareholder can keep the preferred stock or convert it to common stock.

Similarly, convertible bond owners can choose to convert a bond into a specific number of shares of common stock. If your goal is to generate income, you might hold onto the bond and collect interest payments. An investor focusing on growth may convert the bond into shares of common stock.

There are several factors financial advisors review to decide if converting makes sense. For our discussion, I want readers to know that they have the choice- check with a financial advisor for more info.

Buying and selling investments may generate a tax liability.

CHAPTER 21

Realized Gains and Recognized Gains

School shouldn't start until after Labor Day.

Hey — it worked for me.

I'm writing this on August 14th, and school has started (or will start soon) for most kids in the US. Traffic has picked up, parents are busier, and the back-to-school ads have been running for a month.

It's tough for kids to get back into the swing of school. Waking up earlier, homework, after-school activities — it takes a while to adjust.

Most investors don't think about the tax impact of investing until tax time rolls around. Understanding taxes on investments is important because paying taxes reduces your total return on investments.

One tough topic? Realized gains, unrealized gains, and recognized gains.

STARTING WITH REALIZED GAINS AND UNREALIZED GAINS

You need a buy and a sell to generate a realized gain.

You have a realized gain if you buy an asset and sell it for more than you paid for it. If, for example, you buy 100 shares of IBM common stock for $10,000 and sell the shares for $15,000, your realized gain is $5,000.

An unrealized gain has a buy — but no sale. If you buy 100 shares of IBM common stock for $10,000, hold the stock, and the value increases to $17,000, you have an unrealized gain.

Generally speaking, unrealized gains are not taxable.

Here's why.

The value of your investment could also decline. Sure, the IBM investor has a $7,000 unrealized gain right now, but what if the stock price declines to $8,000? It doesn't make sense to tax someone on an unrealized gain, when it could eventually turn into a realized loss.

So, we agree that the investor does not have the dollars from the gain yet, right? No sale, no profit yet.

(There is pending legislation to tax the ultra-wealthy on unrealized gains. I'm ignoring that because the proposal doesn't apply to most investors).

What about losses?

Same deal. You need a buy and sell to generate a realized loss. If you purchase Microsoft stock at $50 and it declines to $38, you have an unrealized loss- and there's no tax consequence.

UNDERSTANDING RECOGNIZED GAINS AND LOSSES

The phrase "recognized" means that the gain or loss is reported on your tax return. In chapter 13, Sally our investor decided to start contributing to her company's 401(k) plan. Most retirement plans- including 401(k) plans- are not taxed until the investor withdraws funds at retirement.

It makes sense because the investor can accumulate a larger retirement plan balance without annual taxes on gains.

Now, if Sally opened a brokerage account (ex. Schwab) that wasn't part of a retirement plan, the gains on stock sales would be taxable each year.

THE LESSON

Gains on stock sales in a retirement plan are not taxed each year. Funding a retirement plan with this tax benefit allows you to accumulate more wealth over time.

CHAPTER 22

Stock Index Gains and Losses

The 2024 Presidential race may be decided by 15 counties in battleground states, according to the US News.

That's 15 out of 3,143 counties in the US, less than one-half of 1% of the total.

There are situations in the stock market when a small number of stocks have a big impact on the rate of return for an entire stock index. Many financial advisors recommend investing in stock index funds, so investors need to know about this possibility.

WHAT IS THE NASDAQ 100?

The NASDAQ 100 is a stock market index like the S&P 500 discussed earlier.

Specifically, this index has 100 equity securities issued by 100 of the largest non-financial companies listed on the NASDAQ stock exchange. It is a modified capitalization-weighted index.

Let's break that down.

STOCK INDEX GAINS AND LOSSES

This index includes stocks from many industries, including industrial, tech, retail, telecom, biotech, and healthcare.

CNBC reported that, as of 7/20/23, the index has a 37% year-to-date return.

Great, right?

Well, hang on...

"The three biggest names appear to account for more than 30% of the index combined."

What?!

On 7/20/23, Microsoft made up 12.67% of the total index, and Apple was 12.31%.

Truly the stock market cool kids.

How does this happen?

Well, the big tech stocks generate huge revenue and profits, more investors buy the stocks, and the total market capitalization (number of shares outstanding times share price) becomes massive.

The result?

These high performers became the biggest percentage of the index.

WHY STOCK DIVERSIFICATION MATTERS

OK, so what's wrong with getting most of the return out of a few stocks?

Because those few large stocks could also produce the *bulk of the losses.*

The reason to own a stock index fund (which invests to mirror an index) is to benefit from diversification. For example, if retail sector stocks decline due to bad news, you own stocks in other industries.

WHAT TO DO NEXT

The good news is that NASDAQ rebalanced the index to provide more diversification.

From the same CNBC article:

"NASDAQ said a special rebalance can be used to 'address overconcentration in the index by redistributing the weights.' The index is rebalanced quarterly to maintain diversification.

The special rebalance fixed a situation where issuers with individual weights above 4.5% account for more than 48% of the total index, as detailed in NASDAQ's methodology.

The limit is designed so that index funds tracking the NASDAQ 100 do not run afoul of regulatory rules governing the diversification of registered investment companies."

Regulators require diversification in the index fund because it reduces investing risks for fund owners.

One more thing.

Discuss these issues with a financial advisor. Ask your advisor to provide a list of the top 10 holdings in the fund, along with the percentages of the stock's value in the fund. Ask questions about diversification.

Why, exactly, are you investing? I'll talk about investment objectives next.

CHAPTER 23

Investment Objectives

Starbucks replaced its CEO in August of 2024.

The reason?

Complexity

According to CNBC: "It's become a familiar sight at Starbucks cafes: a counter crowded with mobile orders, frustrated customers waiting for the drinks they ordered and overwhelmed baristas trying to keep up with it all."

All those customized orders require more time, and tracking costs is far more difficult. We've all heard of that three-sentence specialty order from a Starbucks customer.

"While add-ons like cold foam or syrups are more profitable for Starbucks, they tend to take up more of baristas' time, frustrating both them and customers."

Two problems with complexity

When you have too many options, deciding is more difficult. A flood of options also makes it hard to identify the **right decision**.

The same issues apply to investing. You need a filter to make an informed investment decision.

Your investment objective is a useful filter.

INVESTMENT OBJECTIVE: THREE COMPONENTS

Financial advisors must discuss investment objectives with clients and document the conversation. This step helps the financial advisor to recommend investments that fit the customer's goals.

If you invest directly in mutual funds without an advisor, note that each fund must have a specific investment objective stated in the prospectus (a document given to all investors for disclosure purposes).

Before you invest, consider these three factors:

- **Time horizon**: How long are you investing for? Are you saving money to buy a house in five years? Maybe retiring in 20 years? Be clear about your time horizon, because that will impact how much you're willing to pay to invest- and how much risk you're willing to take.

- **Risk tolerance**: If the value of your investment portfolio declined 20% in one year, is that something you could live with? How about 10%? When most people think of investment risk, they first consider the upside- the possible gains. In my view, your first consideration should be the possible losses. The longer you have to invest, the more time you have to make up for any losses.

- **Your time investment**: How much time are you willing to invest to monitor the performance of your mutual funds- and consider making changes? If investments are new to you, you'll have to invest more time to understand the process. If you don't have a lot of time- or if you're inexperienced- consider paying a fee to an investment advisor who can track the performance of your portfolio.

In chapter 17, Sally the investor decided to invest in a portfolio with 70% stocks and 30% bonds. She is saving for retirement and is taking a moderate amount of risk. Sally relies on her advisor and does not want to research investments.

Think carefully about your investment objective and discuss it with an investment advisor.

You have to consider the cost of any purchase- including investments.

CHAPTER 24

Mutual Fund Costs

In 2024, rising grocery prices are a big issue.

Here's a great statistic from Yahoo Finance:

"During the last federal election on Nov. 3, 2020, food inflation was running at just 3.9% annually. Fast forward to March 2024, and the latest data shows food prices have risen a whopping 25.8% since then. To put that in perspective, a basket of groceries that cost $100 in November 2020 would now set you back $125.80. That's an increase of nearly $26 for the exact same food items."

When consumers pay more for groceries, they have less money for other needs. Discretionary spending that individuals can control, such as entertainment, may be reduced to pay for groceries.

THE IMPACT OF INVESTMENT COSTS

The grocery price issue relates to the problem of investment costs. Investment fees reduce your investment returns, and it's important to understand and minimize investment costs.

The cost to buy and sell individual stocks has declined sharply in recent decades. However, mutual fund costs can put a dent in your investment returns over time. Let's review some details about Sally and her investing:

- Sally decided to invest in a 401(k) retirement plan through her employer (chapter 13)

- Her growth portfolio allocates 70% to stocks, and 30% to bonds (chapter 17)

- Sally is saving for retirement and is willing to take a moderate amount of investing risk (chapter 23)

Sallys' investment advisor recommends the Washington Mutual Fund for the growth portion of her portfolio. The fund invests in large US stocks that may pay dividends and increase in price.

MUTUAL FUND COSTS: 3 TYPES

There are three types of mutual fund costs:

- **Front-end sales charge**: Investors may pay a sales charge when they purchase a mutual fund. A common sales charge level is 5.75%. However, investors may be able to reduce or eliminate the sale charge- more on that below.

- **Annual expenses**: Each fund charges an annual fee to cover the costs of operating the fund. Pay close attention to the annual expense. It's charged every year and a high annual expense can eat into your investment returns over time.

- **Back-end sales charge**: A fund may assess a sales charge when you withdraw funds.

If you stay invested for 5-7 years or more, you may be able to avoid both a front-end and a back-end sales charge. The idea here is to reward buyers for long-term investing. If you can avoid all sales charges, your only cost is the annual expense.

MORNINGSTAR:
A MUTUAL FUND RATINGS TOOL

Morningstar is a great site for mutual fund performance information. You can find research and current stories on mutual funds and a link to the fund's prospectus, which is an SEC-reviewed document that provides disclosure to investors.

I'd recommend working with a financial advisor as a first priority. If you decide you want to do extra homework on your mutual funds, check out Morningstar.

CHAPTER 25

Mutual Fund Performance

Fantasy football has made the most popular sport in the US (the NFL) even more popular.

Businesses like ESPN provide hundreds (maybe thousands) of player stats to support fantasy football. These stats are updated with real-time game results.

The mutual fund industry also provides tons of data. If you watch CNBC, you may be overwhelmed by the amount of finance data provided. Every commercial break includes mutual fund companies promoting their funds.

So how do you distinguish one fund's performance from another?

I'll address that now, using the Washington Mutual fund as an example.

AMERICAN FUNDS WASHINGTON MUTUAL INVESTORS FUND

Washington Mutual is one of the oldest and largest mutual funds. It focuses on stocks issued by large, US-based companies. Morningstar has a fund ratings system from 1 to 5, so I picked a fund with a 4-star rating. I chose an expense ratio that was in the low range (less than or equal to 1%) and used that as a filter also. Here are some of the important features of this fund:

- **The bluest of the blue chips:** Blue chip stocks are large companies with recognizable names — firms that sell products that you buy all the time. Think Proctor and Gamble, the people who make Crest toothpaste and dozens of other products. Because these companies have large brands and a big market share, they can generate consistent sales and earnings. So, over time, the stock price can increase- but slowly.

- **Performance:** It's a standard practice for a fund company to list their performance over the most recent 1, 5, and 10 years. You'll note on the first page of the website that performance is "net of fees" (after the annual expense is subtracted).

- **Investment objective:** Read the fund's objective and see if it matches your personal investment objective. This fund's objective is to produce income (through dividend payments) and to provide an opportunity for growth of principal (your original investment is the principal) that is consistent with sound common stock investing. Slow and steady- and not flashy.

Now, if this fund doesn't meet your needs, use the Morningstar Fund Screener tool to find a stock fund that takes more risk- or maybe a fund that invests in bonds.

You now have the tools to find great-performing mutual funds. However, I highly recommend consulting a financial advisor before making any final decisions.

CHAPTER 26

Exchange Traded Funds

It's nearly September 1st, and most schools are back in session.

My mother taught for nearly 40 years; many friends and relatives are teachers. The best instructors figure out a way to teach a particular topic and stick with it year after year.

The best learning tool I've ever seen?

Schoolhouse Rock!

CONJUNCTION JUNCTION, WHAT'S YOUR FUNCTION?

Schoolhouse Rock! was a series of 65 educational short films originally aired on Saturday mornings in the '70s and '80s. The series was revived in later years, and you can now find the series on the Disney Plus streaming app.

Do these songs ring a bell?

- "I'm Just a Bill" (explains how legislation moves through Congress)

- "Conjunction Junction" (reviewed how conjunctions are used in grammar)

I still remember the songs — this concept has worked for decades.

A concept that has served investors well for years is exchange-traded funds (ETFs).

UNDERSTANDING ETFS

The Standard and Poor's (S&P) 500 index was discussed in Chapter 13. It's a stock market index tracking the stock performance of 500 of the largest companies listed on US stock exchanges.

Investing in the S&P 500 index offers these benefits:

- **Diversified portfolio**: Multiple industries

- **Large companies** that may generate consistent earnings

- **Rebalancing**: This concept is explained in chapter 22. Rebalancing prevents one stock from making up a big percentage of the total portfolio. Investors stay diversified

OK, assume that you want to invest in the S&P 500 index. How?

Use an exchange-traded fund that invests in the S&P 500 index. Here's how ETFs work:

- **Stock index tool**: An exchange-traded fund (ETF) can track an underlying stock index.

- **Low cost**: ETFs are listed on exchanges and are a low-cost choice.

- **Liquidity**: ETF shares trade throughout the day just like ordinary stock, and you can sell an ETF anytime the stock exchanges are open.

In Chapter 25, I used the Washington Mutual fund as an example. The annual expense for an ETF may be much lower than a mutual fund's expense. The commission on an ETF may also be much lower than the sales charge you pay for a mutual fund.

Ask an investment advisor if choosing an ETF instead of a mutual fund will lower your total costs over the long term.

CHAPTER 27

Bond Mutual Funds

Cowboys Wide Receiver Cee Dee Lamb "got the bag."

In late August of 2024, Lamb signed a 4-year, $136 million deal. According to ESPN, the deal includes a $38 million signing bonus, the largest ever given to a wide receiver, and $100 million guaranteed, per sources.

How confident is Cee Dee Lamb that he'll get paid?

Pretty confident.

As Sportico points out: "Each of the 32 NFL teams received just over $400 million from the league office for the 2023 season, according to multiple people familiar with the league's finances who were not authorized to speak publicly." That does not include the Cowboy's ticket sales.

What other costs do the Dallas Cowboys have to cover?

"In 2023, the NFL salary cap was $224.8 million, with each club also on the hook for nine figures worth of player benefits, stadium costs, and team expenses."

NFL teams have more than enough revenue to cover expenses.

You can use this same concept to analyze bond investments.

SECURED AND UNSECURED BONDS

As I explained in chapter 9, you can invest in secured and unsecured bonds:

- **Secured bond**: A secured bond may be backed by specific assets, such as a building or equipment. If the bond issuer misses principal or interest payments, the assets can be sold to repay the bondholders.

- **Unsecured bond**: An unsecured bond is backed by the issuer's ability to pay. Think of an unsecured credit card: repayment is based on the card owner's ability to repay, not with specific assets.

US Treasury bonds are unsecured bonds backed by the federal government's ability to raise revenue to repay the bonds. Treasury bonds carry the highest credit rating, even though the bond is not secured.

Why?

Because the federal government can raise taxes to fund bond repayments.

BOND CREDIT RATINGS

Bond ratings measure a bond issuer's ability to repay all interest and principal payments on time. There are several private independent rating agencies- I'll use the Standard & Poor's rating system.

Standard & Poor's rates bonds on a scale from AAA down to D. US Treasuries, for example, are rated AAA. The rating would be in the C or D range if a bond issuer is close to defaulting (not paying) on required principal and interest payments.

Investment grade bonds are assigned a AAA to BBB- rating from Standard & Poor's. Many financial services pros only recommend investment-grade bonds.

In chapter 27, you learned that Sally invested in her 401(k) plan with 70% in stocks and 30% in bonds. I'll assume the bond portion is invested in Vanguard's Intermediate-Term Investment Grade bond fund.

Bond mutual funds are used along with stock mutual funds to create a portfolio that balances income and growth objectives.

CHAPTER 28

Working with Bond Premiums, and Bond Discounts

It's late August 2024, and the Federal Reserve is proposing interest rate cuts as the economy slows down. Lower interest rates reduce borrowing costs for businesses and consumers. The hope is that lower interest rates will increase economic activity.

What's the impact on bond investors?

INTEREST RATES AND BOND PRICES

In chapter 27, you learned that Sally invested in a Vanguard Investment Grade Bond mutual fund. The Vanguard portfolio manager can hold bonds until maturity or sell bonds before they mature. An interest rate cut impacts the price received when a bond is sold, generating a gain or loss in the fund.

UNDERSTANDING A BOND PREMIUM

Assume that Vanguard owns a $10,000 6% AA-rated IBM corporate bond due in 10 years. When interest rates decline, the 6% 10-year bond is more valuable.

Why?

103

New AA-rated 10-year bonds (for IBM or other corporations) will be issued at a lower interest rate. That makes sense because the issuer wants to pay no more than the market rate for interest. Assume that new AA-rated 10-year bonds have a 5.5% interest rate.

The 10-year 6% bond price will increase because the interest rate is higher than current market rates. When a bond is priced at more than the face amount ($10,000), it sells at a premium.

The Vanguard money manager may sell the $10,000 bond for $10,500 and generate a $500 gain for the mutual fund.

CONSIDERING A BOND DISCOUNT

Now consider the flip side: interest rates increase.

The $10,000 6% AA-rated IBM corporate bond due in 10 years is <u>less valuable</u>. Newly issued AA-rated 10-year bonds have a <u>higher interest rate than 6%</u>. Think of it this way: if you can own a bond paying 6% or 9%, you rather earn 9%. The 6% bond is less attractive because it pays less interest.

When a bond is priced at less than the face amount ($10,000), it sells at a discount.

The Vanguard money manager may sell the $10,000 bond for $980 and generate a $20 loss for the mutual fund.

If you own a bond mutual fund, the fund manager may not hold all of the bonds until maturity. The fund may incur capital gains and losses if the portfolio manager sells bonds. The gains and losses are reported to investors and may impact your tax return.

Your ability to borrow has a big impact on your personal finances.

CHAPTER 29

The Importance of Credit Scores

It's the first weekend of college football, and fan complaints about referees are already happening. Maybe the toughest referee call is passing interference.

I saw a Penn State receiver and a West Virginia defensive back get tangled up as they both went up for the ball. The receiver pushed the defensive back's arms off his shoulder and made the catch. However, the receiver pushed so hard that the defensive back fell and couldn't try for the ball.

Which player should be called for pass interference?

Even with instant replay, it's hard to say.

Calculating your credit score involves hard numbers and some judgments made by the refs at the credit bureaus. You can take steps to improve your credit score.

FACTORS THAT IMPACT YOUR CREDIT SCORE

If you have a poor credit score, the impact on your finances can be substantial. Your options to obtain credit and pay a reasonable interest rate are limited. Many people with poor credit cannot obtain a loan at all.

These factors impact your credit score.

- **Payment history**: Making debt payments on time.

- **Amount of debt**: How much debt do you have outstanding? That may include a home loan, car loans, student loans, and credit card debt.

- **Credit applications**: If a lender performs a hard credit check, the check will reduce your credit score slightly. If you apply for loans frequently, you're viewed as a higher credit risk.

Here's a factor many borrowers don't consider- credit utilization rate.

The term refers to the percentage of your total available credit that you use. Assume you have a $5,000 credit limit on a credit card and have a $1,000 balance. Your credit utilization rate is ($1,000 / $5,000), or 20%.

To maintain a strong credit rating, experts recommend you limit credit use to 20% of your available credit. Many consumers get approved for credit and run up the balance near the credit limit. That approach hurts your credit score.

WORKING ON YOUR CREDIT RATING

Fortunately, there are steps you can take to improve your credit rating.

One of those steps is to borrow more money.

Now, that doesn't make sense on the surface. Many individuals developed a poor credit rating *precisely* because they borrowed more money. But just as borrowing (and messing things up) hurts your credit score, taking out a loan and paying it back as planned improves your credit rating.

The difference-maker is creating a budget for the loan payment. I talked about budgeting in chapter 5. The goal is to take out a reasonable amount of debt and pay it back on time.

CHECK YOUR CREDIT SCORE

Good credit activity is just as important as avoiding credit mistakes. Your credit score can improve when lenders report on-time payments to credit bureaus.

Check your credit report periodically to verify that your good credit activity is correctly stated on your credit history. Contact the lender if a loan payoff or timely payments are not listed.

Over time, you'll gain the satisfaction of building a great credit rating.

Credit card use can be expensive if you don't do your homework.

CHAPTER 30

Unexpected Credit Card Fees

My street was blocked for construction, and cars needed to turn in front of my house as a detour. So how do you communicate the detour to drivers?

At first, someone taped a handwritten sign to an orange cone that read: "Road Closed. Not kidding. Turn here and turn around."

Not really effective.

The city finally came by with a large sign that drivers could read.

Rushing to do anything creates problems.

When approved for a new credit card, read the disclosures on the credit card issuer's website and review the credit card agreement carefully.

Credit card issuers often have details in the fine print that can cost you.

UNEXPECTED FEES AND PENALTIES

I've written frequently on credit cards for both individuals and businesses. Here are some of the sneaky policies that can generate problems for consumers:

- **Penalty APR (interest) rate:** If you're late on a payment or go over your credit limit, your card issuer may charge a penalty interest rate. The higher rate may be charged for up to 12 months.

- **Card spending requirements:** Some card issuers require you to use at least 30% (or more) of your credit limit. If you spend less, you pay additional fees or miss out on card rewards.

- **Lost rewards:** Several card issuers force cardholders to wait 12 months before they can redeem rewards.

Sneaky, right?!

Here are some steps you can take to make informed decisions regarding credit cards.

CREDIT CARD STRATEGIES

- **Read the entire, boring agreement:** Yes, it's dull, and you're probably tempted to throw the agreement in the trash- but read it. Recent changes in federal law have forced credit card issuers to make agreements easier to read, but it's still a struggle. Read the whole thing and take some notes- particularly about payment due dates.

- **Pay a day early, even online:** Don't take the risk of paying late, so pay a day early, and ONLY pay online. Mail is too unreliable and makes it difficult to prove that a payment was made on time.

- **Pay in full, every time, or don't get a card:** In my view, the only reason to get a credit card is to use credit wisely and build your credit rating. Don't use credit cards if you can't pay the card in full every month. The interest rates are simply too high to justify carrying a balance.

- **Only use a card that earns points:** You can find credit cards that offer airline, hotel, or purchase points.

- **Balance transfers:** OK- you can certainly find a card that's willing to take you as a client in exchange for a lower, "teaser" interest rate. But, like I said- *don't carry a balance.*

When in doubt, get a customer service rep on the line to clarify card policies.

CHAPTER 31

Reviewing Taxes on Investments

Is your school banning phones?

It's a growing trend.

According to a June 2024 USA Today article: "Three states recently passed laws banning or restricting cell phone use in schools. Florida was the first to do so in 2023."

Why?

Sensory overload.

You can't focus on learning about the American Revolution (I loved history) or Physics (science classes were a drag) while bombarded with social media posts at school.

It's simply too much to take in.

Understanding the tax code is also challenging. There's too much information, and it's so overwhelming that most people throw up their hands and avoid tax issues.

To understand personal finances, you need some basic tax knowledge.

REVIEWING TAXES ON INVESTMENTS

TWO INVESTMENTS

Sally invests in her company's 401(k) plan (chapter 13). Here are some details about the investment:

- **Asset allocation model**: Sally chose a growth portfolio with 70% invested in stocks and 30% contributed to a bond portfolio (chapter 17).

- **Mutual funds**: The growth portion of the portfolio is invested in Washington Mutual Fund (chapter 24), and Sally uses a Vanguard Investment Grade bond fund (chapter 27).

- **Tax deferral**: If Sally leaves the dollars invested in the 401(k) plan, she is not taxed on the income and profits until she withdraws money at retirement (chapter 14).

Sally also inherits 200 shares of Apple common stock. Her accountant tells her that the cost basis on the stock is $50 per share. Cost basis refers to the cost used to determine a gain or loss on a sale. If you inherit investments, talk with an accountant about cost basis.

During the year, Sally sells 30 shares at $60 per share. Her gain is:

- $60 sales proceeds - $50 cost basis = $10 X 30 shares = $300 gain

Sally earned $100 in cash dividends on the Apple stock.

What is the tax liability for these investments?

TAX ON INVESTMENTS

As stated previously Sally does not pay taxes on dividends, interest, or capital gains on the 401(k) investment. The Apple stock produces two types of tax:

- **Capital gain**: Sally pays tax on the $300 capital gain
- **Cash dividends**: The $100 in dividends is also taxable

Where are these transactions posted on Sally's tax return?

The $300 capital gain and the $100 dividend increase Sally's taxable income. Sally's taxable gross wages total $96,000 (chapter 13). The investment activity increases her taxable income to $96,400. If the tax rate is 25%, Sally's tax liability is:

- $96,400 taxable income X 25% tax rate = $24,100 tax liability

Sally pays the tax liability through tax withholdings on her salary. She may pay additional taxes when she files her tax return if the withholdings don't cover the entire tax liability.

WHY RETIREMENT PLAN DISTRIBUTIONS ARE IMPORTANT

How you take money out of a retirement plan is just as important as investing in the plan. Your decisions have a big impact on how much you can withdraw, and the taxes you'll pay on distributions.

Assume, for example, that Sally has $100 invested and the amount grows to $300 in 20 years. None of those dollars have been taxed yet. So, when Sally starts taking money out for retirement, the entire $300 balance is taxed as she makes withdrawals.

Work with a CPA and a financial advisor to understand the retirement plan dollars you must withdraw each year and the tax impact of each withdrawal

UNDERSTANDING THE GIFT TAX

The tax code allows taxpayers to gift (give away) a limited amount of money each year, and there is no tax on the gift. If you stay within the limit, you don't have to file a gift tax return or pay taxes on the gift.

So how much can you give away?

According to NerdWallet, the 2024 gift tax exclusion is $18,000, meaning that you can gift up to $18,000 *per recipient* and not file a gift tax return. If you're married, each spouse can give away $18,000 per recipient without incurring the gift tax.

What's the tax strategy behind gifting dollars each year?

It reduces the size of your estate, which lowers the amount of estate tax that a taxpayer may have to pay when he or she passes away.

WORKING WITH THE ESTATE TAX

A definition from NerdWallet:

"The federal estate tax is a tax that's levied on a dead person's inherited assets. The estate tax ranges from rates of 18% to 40% and generally only applies to assets over $13.61 million in 2024."

As you can see, the estate tax does not apply to most people. However, if you're accumulating wealth, gifting money each year lowers the size of your estate.

Work with a CPA or a tax preparer and ask questions about taxes on your investments.

CHAPTER 32

Tax Deduction Limitations

Every time we have a Presidential Debate — or any political debate — we hear the media talk about fact-checking.

Was the politician's statement accurate?

It's important to know.

The same is true of tax deductions.

Many taxpayers have a vague idea that medical expenses, mortgage interest, and other spending are deductible. When you dig a little deeper, you find out that some deductions are limited.

Let's cover some common tax deductions and how much you can deduct.

UNDERSTANDING SCHEDULE A

Some common deductions are calculated on Schedule A of your personal tax return (Form 1040). The 1040 has several schedules that you may need to complete, depending on your finances during the year.

I'm using the draft of Schedule A for tax year 2024- The form is not yet finalized as I write. The tax rules may change slightly, but you'll get a general idea of how the deductions work.

Adjusted gross income (AGI) is used to calculate the limits on several tax deductions. Think of AGI as the total income you earn from all sources. Wages, interest income, dividend payments, and gains on investment sales are included in AGI.

In chapter 31, you read that Sally had adjusted gross income of $96,400. That includes her work salary, cash dividends, and a capital gain on a stock sale.

WORKING WITH MEDICAL EXPENSES

In 2024, Sally's medical and dental expense deduction is limited to 7.5% of AGI. The total amount she can deduct is:

- $96,400 AGI X 7.5% = $7,230

CONSIDERING THE STATE AND LOCAL TAX DEDUCTION

Taxpayers can deduct state and local taxes on the federal (IRS) tax return, but the current amount is limited to $10,000 for a single taxpayer.

I'll assume that Sally pays a 6% state tax rate. Here is her state tax deduction:

- $96,400 AGI X 6% = $5,784

Sally can deduct the entire state tax balance plus additional local taxes up to $10,000.

Many high-income earners in states with a high state tax rate (California and New York, for example) cannot deduct all their state and local taxes.

DEDUCTING MORTGAGE INTEREST

Your home loan interest is deductible. Currently, there is no limit on the mortgage interest deduction.

Assume that you pay $18,000 in interest on your home loan. Current IRS rules allow you to deduct the $18,000 using Schedule A.

HOW DOES THE SCHEDULE A DEDUCTION IMPACT THE 1040 TAX RETURN?

Every taxpayer is allowed to take the standard deduction, and the standard deduction may be higher or lower than your itemized deductions.

Sally compares the total itemized deductions on Schedule A to the standard deduction for a single taxpayer ($14,600 in 2024). If the itemized deductions are *more* than the standard deduction, she uses the itemized deductions total. Otherwise, Sally takes the $14,600 standard deduction.

Have a CPA or tax preparer complete your tax return. Keep accurate spending records so you can maximize your itemized deductions.

CHAPTER 33

The Myth of Cheap Insurance

There is no such thing as "cheap insurance".

Instead, there is low-cost insurance that doesn't provide the same level of benefit as more expensive insurance.

Why?

Because managing an insurance business is mostly about math.

PREDICTING INSURANCE CLAIMS

Insurance companies hire hundreds of actuaries — math majors who use data to model risk and uncertainty. Actuaries analyze large groups of life insurance policyholders and project the likelihood that an insured person will pass away.

It's a similar process for car insurance.

Given a large group of car insurance policyholders, what is the likelihood that an insured person will have an accident?

The cost of an insurance claim varies based on the make and model of the car, the amount of damage, and other factors.

Why is car insurance more expensive for drivers under age 25?

On average, young drivers have more accidents.

USING HISTORICAL DATA

All of this analysis over decades gives insurance companies the ability to build precise prediction models. A trend of more hurricanes in Florida? Home insurance premiums increase. Traffic in Seattle getting more congested? Car insurance premiums rise.

Get insurance quotes to test my theory. Here's an example.

TEST DRIVING THE CHEAP INSURANCE ISSUE

My son lives in New York and is self-employed, so I went to the state's website that offers health insurance. The New York site is affiliated with the Affordable Care Act's national program. I generated three different quotes for health insurance.

What did I find?

The quote with the lowest monthly premiums had the highest deductible and the least coverage. If you're willing to pay higher premiums, you can get a lower deductible and more coverage.

HOMEOWNERS INSURANCE POLICIES

Bankrate explained four situations that are not typically covered under a standard homeowners insurance policy:

- **Flooding**: This situation may surprise you, since flooding is fairly common. Most people think that flooding is covered in a homeowners policy, but damage due to flooding is not normally covered. Fortunately, the federal government advertises flood insurance coverage options through the FloodSmart.gov site.

- **Mold**: The Center for Disease Control and Prevention points out that some people experience breathing problems due to mold. Your homeowners insurance policy will typically offer limited coverage for mold- or exclude coverage completely. Side note: If you have trouble with allergies, I use an air purifier- really helps.

- **Sewer Lines**: Many cities are not properly maintaining sewer lines, and these lines are at risk of backing up, due to the aging infrastructure. The lines are designed to handle both stormwater and raw sewage. A sewer line backup can damage your home's structure (floors, walls, electrical systems). The backup can also damage furniture and other valuables in your home.

- **Renters Insurance:** A final point for people who rent property. You landlord's homeowners insurance on your rented property does not cover anything *inside the structure*. To cover your personal property, ask an insurance agent about a renters insurance policy.

To ensure that you have coverage for these issues, you can add an endorsement to your homeowners policy. Your insurance premiums will be more expensive, but you'll have coverage. Consult with a licensed insurance agent who understands your state's insurance laws, as these laws can differ between states.

INSURANCE IS SIMPLY A MATH PROBLEM

I love Geico and Progressive ads, but "saving hundreds on insurance" comes with higher premiums and less coverage. Check with an insurance agent to understand the pros and cons of insurance costs.

CHAPTER 34

Reviewing the Personal Finance Journey

"If you don't know where you are going, any road will get you there." (Alice in Wonderland).

I've always loved this quote from author Lewis Carroll, and I've certainly done my share of wandering with no real direction. But I hope this book sets you on the road to a better personal finance outcome.

Let's review what happened along Sally's journey.

Sally set up a budget with $300 a month in savings. She invested the $300 a month in her employer's 401(k) retirement plan, which added a $15 (5%) matching contribution.

She learned how stocks, bonds, mutual funds, and exchange-traded funds (ETFs) work, and the risks of investing in each security.

Sally decided to take a moderate amount of investing risk with an asset allocation of 70% in stocks and 30% in bonds. She invested in a stock mutual fund and a bond fund. Sally also inherited 200 shares of Apple common stock.

She reviewed the pros and cons of using credit cards, and how a credit score is calculated.

At the end of the year, Sally paid taxes on Apple stock dividends and a capital gain when she sold some of her Apple shares. She has a general idea of how medical expenses, state taxes, and mortgage interest are deducted on Schedule A of her federal tax return.

Sally is on track to maintain an emergency fund, grow her retirement account, and reach her financial goals

So where do you go from here?

Find a financial advisor, a tax preparer, and an insurance agent with industry experience, and listen carefully to their advice. Perhaps most importantly, don't let the constant stream of finance news distract you from your personal finance goals.

Thanks for reading — best of luck!

-Ken

About the Author

Kenneth W. Boyd, a former CPA, has over 40 years of experience in accounting, education, and financial services.

He is a writer, editor, and video content provider on business topics. Ken has written for Investopedia, QuickBooks, Stampli.com, Rho.co, and Ramp.com, among others.

Boyd is the author of *Cost Accounting for Dummies*, *Accounting All-In-One for Dummies*, *The CPA Exam for Dummies*, and *1,001 Accounting Questions for Dummies*. He has worked as an auditor, tax preparer, and accounting professor. His YouTube channel (kenboydstl) has hundreds of videos on accounting and finance.

Ken lives in St. Louis, Missouri, with his wife, Patty. Their three children, Kaitlin, Connor, and Meaghan, have all left the nest and started their careers.

Acknowledgments

Thanks to my agent Matt Wagner of Fresh Books Literary Agency, who found my YouTube channel and gave me my start as a writer. I owe a huge debt of thanks to Barry Schoenborn and Joe Kraynak, who served as the Technical Writers for my first two books. Their wit, wisdom, and work ethic helped me become a better writer.

I also want to thank Alan and Ian at The Book Designers, who created a beautiful cover and the book's interior. Thank you to my editor (and daughter) Meaghan Boyd. Finally, thanks to my dear friend Dave Pannell and the picnic table conversation that changed my career path.

Made in the USA
Monee, IL
16 December 2024